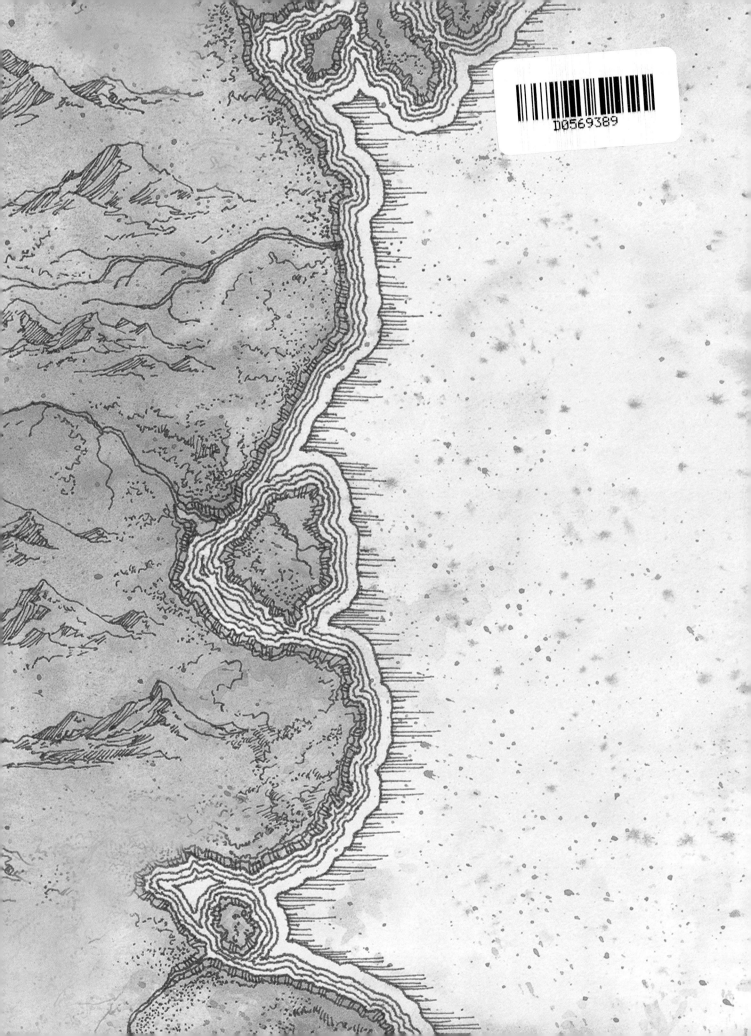

My World

Series Authors
Dr. Richard G. Boehm
Claudia Hoone
Dr. Thomas M. McGowan
Dr. Mabel C. McKinney-Browning
Dr. Ofelia B. Miramontes

Consultants for Primary Grades
Carol Hamilton Cobb
Janet J. Eubank
Billie M. Kapp

Series Consultants
Dr. Alma Flor Ada
Dr. Phillip Bacon
Dr. W. Dorsey Hammond
Dr. Asa Grant Hilliard, III

HARCOURT BRACE & COMPANY

Orlando Atlanta Austin Boston San Francisco Chicago Dallas
New York Toronto London

SERIES AUTHORS

Dr. Richard G. Boehm
Professor
Department of Geography and
  Planning
Southwest Texas State University
San Marcos, Texas

Claudia Hoone
Teacher
Ralph Waldo Emerson School #58
Indianapolis, Indiana

Dr. Thomas M. McGowan
Associate Professor
Division of Curriculum and
  Instruction
Arizona State University
Tempe, Arizona

Dr. Mabel C. McKinney-Browning
Director
Division for Public Education
American Bar Association
Chicago, Illinois

Dr. Ofelia B. Miramontes
Associate Professor
School of Education
University of Colorado
Boulder, Colorado

SERIES CONSULTANTS

Dr. Alma Flor Ada
Professor
School of Education
University of San Francisco
San Francisco, California

Dr. Phillip Bacon
Professor Emeritus of Geography
  and Anthropology
University of Houston
Houston, Texas

Dr. W. Dorsey Hammond
Professor of Education
Oakland University
Rochester, Michigan

Dr. Asa Grant Hilliard, III
Fuller E. Callaway Professor of
  Urban Education
Georgia State University
Atlanta, Georgia

MEDIA AND LITERATURE SPECIALISTS

Dr. Joseph A. Braun, Jr.
Professor of Elementary
  Social Studies
Department of Curriculum and
  Instruction
Illinois State University
Normal, Illinois

Meredith McGowan
Youth Librarian
Tempe Public Library
Tempe, Arizona

GRADE-LEVEL CONSULTANTS AND REVIEWERS

Arlene Adams
Teacher
Highland Village Elementary School
Lewisville, Texas

Carol Hamilton Cobb
Teacher
Gateway School
Metropolitan Nashville Public
  Schools
Madison, Tennessee

Janet J. Eubank
Language Arts Curriculum
  Specialist
Wichita Public Schools
Wichita, Kansas

Billie M. Kapp
Teacher
Coventry Grammar School
Coventry, Connecticut

Robert L. Lichtenberger
Teacher
Hollie Parsons Elementary School
Copperas Cove, Texas

Betty Maxey
Teacher
W. H. Taft Elementary School
Boise, Idaho

Nan Pelletier
Elementary Consulting Teacher
Boise Public Schools
Boise, Idaho

Copyright © 1997 by Harcourt Brace & Company

Requests for permission to make copies of any part of the work should be mailed to: Permissions Department, Harcourt Brace & Company, 6277 Sea Harbor Drive, Orlando, Florida 32887-6777.

HARCOURT BRACE and Quill Design is a registered trademark of Harcourt Brace & Company.

Acknowledgments and other credits appear in the back of this book.

Printed in the United States of America

ISBN: 0-15-302037-7

   4 5 6 7 8 9 10   032   99 98 97

CONTENTS

ATLAS   A1
Map of the World   A2
Map of the United States   A4

UNIT 1   **School Days**   **1**

Set the Scene with Literature
"Good Books, Good Times!"
by Lee Bennett Hopkins   2

Lesson • My Classroom   4

Lesson • Things I Learn   6

Geography Skill
  • Learn from a Picture and a Map   8

Lesson • School Workers   10

Geography Skill
  • Read a Map Key   12

Lesson • We Help One Another   14

Brainstorm   16

Lesson • We Follow School Rules   18

Story Cloth Summary   20

UNIT REVIEW   22

UNIT 2   At Home with My Family   24

Set the Scene with Literature
"Home! You're Where It's Warm Inside"
by Jack Prelutsky   26

Lesson • Welcome Home   28

Geography Skill
• Find a Home Address on a Map   30

Lesson • Learn with Literature
Flower Garden
written by Eve Bunting
illustrated by Kathryn Hewitt   32

Chart and Graph Skill
• Read a Time Line   42

Lesson • Families Make Choices   44

Thinking Skill
• Make a Choice   46

Lesson • Families Long Ago:
A Thanksgiving Story   48

Making Social Studies Real
• Trevor's Campaign for
the Homeless   52

Story Cloth Summary   54

UNIT REVIEW   56

UNIT 3   Living in a Community   58

Set the Scene with Literature
"I Live in a City"
a song by Malvina Reynolds   60

Lesson • Meet My Neighbors   62

Lesson • Community Leaders   66

Geography Skill
• Find Directions on a Map   68

Lesson • Trading Goods
and Services   70

Chart and Graph Skill
• Read a Table   72

Lesson • Getting from Here
to There   74

Making Social Studies Real
• Kids Against Crime   78

Story Cloth Summary   80

UNIT REVIEW   82

UNIT 4   In and Around the Land   84

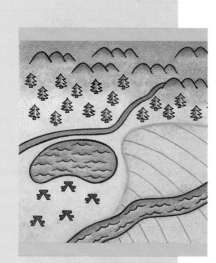

Set the Scene with Literature
"From the Yard of My House"
by F. Isabel Campoy   86

Lesson • Land and Water   88

Geography Skill
• Find Land and Water on a Map   90

Lesson • Our Treasured Resources   92

Lesson • The Cheese Factory   96

Chart and Graph Skill
• Read a Pictograph   100

Lesson • Saving Our Resources   102

Brainstorm   104

Thinking Skill
• Find Out What People Think   106

Story Cloth Summary   108

UNIT REVIEW   110

UNIT 5   My Country, My Heroes   112

Set the Scene with Literature
"The Pledge of Allegiance"   114

Lesson • **Sharing the Land**   116

Lesson • **Two Peoples Meet**   120

Lesson • **Independence Day**   124

Citizenship Skill
• **Make a Choice by Voting**   128

Brainstorm   130

Lesson • **Learn with Literature**
America the Beautiful
written by Katharine Lee Bates
illustrated by Neil Waldman   132

Chart and Graph Skill
• **Read a Diagram**   140

Story Cloth Summary   142

UNIT REVIEW   144

| UNIT 6 | My World Near and Far | 146 |

Set the Scene with Literature

"It's a Small World"
a song by Richard M. Sherman
and Robert B. Sherman — 148

Lesson • Where in the World
Do People Live? — 150

Geography Skill
• Use a Globe — 152

Lesson • People Are People
Everywhere — 154

Lesson • People Everywhere
Are Linked — 158

Chart and Graph Skill
• Use a Bar Graph — 160

Lesson • We Share the Planet — 162

Thinking Skill
• Tell What Might Happen — 166

Making Social Studies Real
• Kids Meeting Kids — 168

Story Cloth Summary — 170

UNIT REVIEW — 172

Glossary — 174

F.Y.I.

Literature and Primary Sources

"Good Books, Good Times!"
a poem by Lee Bennett Hopkins 2
"Home! You're Where It's Warm Inside"
a poem by Jack Prelutsky 26
Flower Garden
written by Eve Bunting 32
"I Live in a City"
a song by Malvina Reynolds 60
"From the Yard of My House"
a poem by F. Isabel Campoy 86
"The Pledge of Allegiance" 114
America the Beautiful
written by Katharine Lee Bates 132
"It's a Small World"
a song by Richard M. and Robert B. Sherman 148

Skills

How to Learn from a Picture and a Map 8
How to Read a Map Key 12
How to Find a Home Address on a Map 30

How to Read a Time Line 42
How to Make a Choice 46
How to Find Directions on a Map 68

How to Read a Table 72
How to Find Land and Water on a Map 90
How to Read a Pictograph 100

How to Find Out What People Think 106
How to Make a Choice by Voting 128
How to Read a Diagram 140

How to Use a Globe 152
How to Use a Bar Graph 160
How to Tell What Might Happen 166

Features

Brainstorm
Classroom Etiquette   16
Protecting the Earth   104
Laws Help People   130

Making Social Studies Real
Trevor's Campaign for the Homeless   52
Kids Against Crime   78
Kids Meeting Kids   168

Maps

Map of the World   A2
Map of the United States   A4
Classroom Map   9
School Map   13
Home Addresses   31
Tiny Town   69
Mountain Lake Park   91
The United States of America   118
Columbus's Route   121
The Globe
    Western Hemisphere   153
    Eastern Hemisphere   153

Charts, Graphs, Diagrams, Tables, and Time Lines

Things I Learn (diagram)   6
Class Rules (list)   18
Anna's Time Line   43
Spending List   44
My Shopping List   70
Goods and Services (table)   73
Land and Water (diagram)   88
Dairy Foods We Ate at Lunch (pictograph)   101
Statue of Liberty (diagram)   141
Spencer's Toys (bar graph)   161

ATLAS

Geo Georgie wants to invite you to visit new places this year. The maps in this book will help you to know where you are. When you see Geo Georgie, stop and learn how to use the maps.

Come back to this Atlas as you journey through Stories in Time.

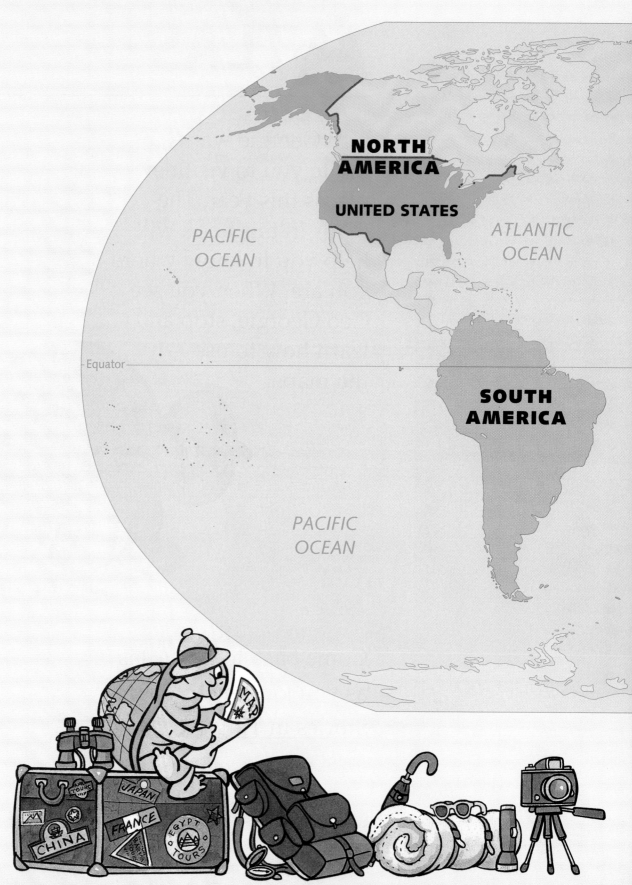

NORTH
AMERICA

UNITED STATES

PACIFIC
OCEAN

ATLANTIC
OCEAN

Equator

SOUTH
AMERICA

PACIFIC
OCEAN

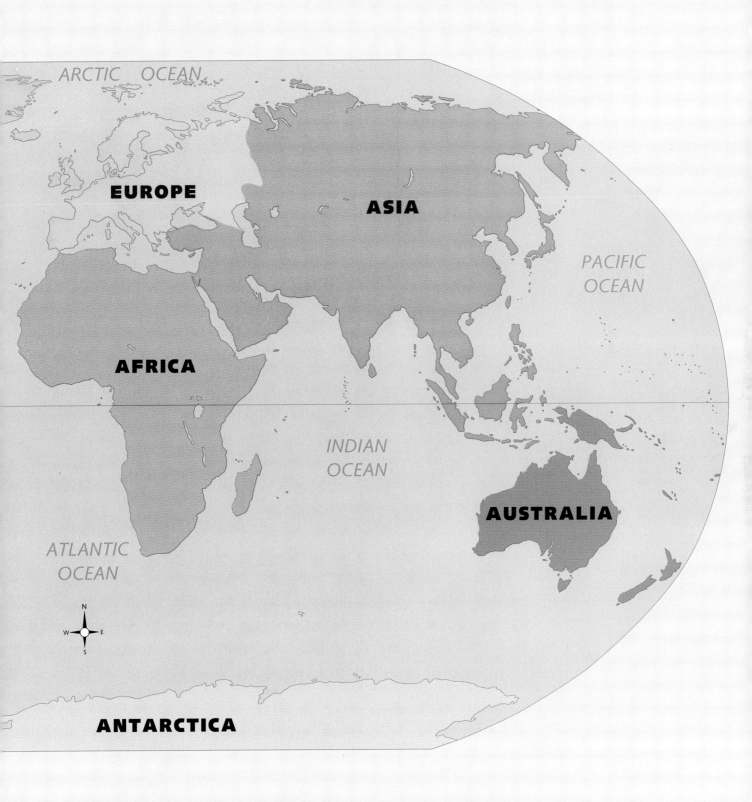

ARCTIC OCEAN

EUROPE

ASIA

PACIFIC OCEAN

AFRICA

INDIAN OCEAN

ATLANTIC OCEAN

AUSTRALIA

N
W • E
S

ANTARCTICA

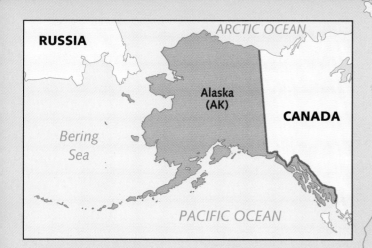

RUSSIA

ARCTIC OCEAN

Alaska
(AK)

CANADA

Bering
Sea

PACIFIC OCEAN

CANADA

Washington
(WA)

Montana
(MT)

Oregon
(OR)

Idaho
(ID)

Wyoming
(WY)

Great
Salt
Lake

Nevada
(NV)

Utah
(UT)

Colorado
(CO)

PACIFIC

OCEAN

California
(CA)

Arizona
(AZ)

New
Mexico
(NM)

Hawaii
(HI)

PACIFIC
OCEAN

MEXICO

N
W E
S

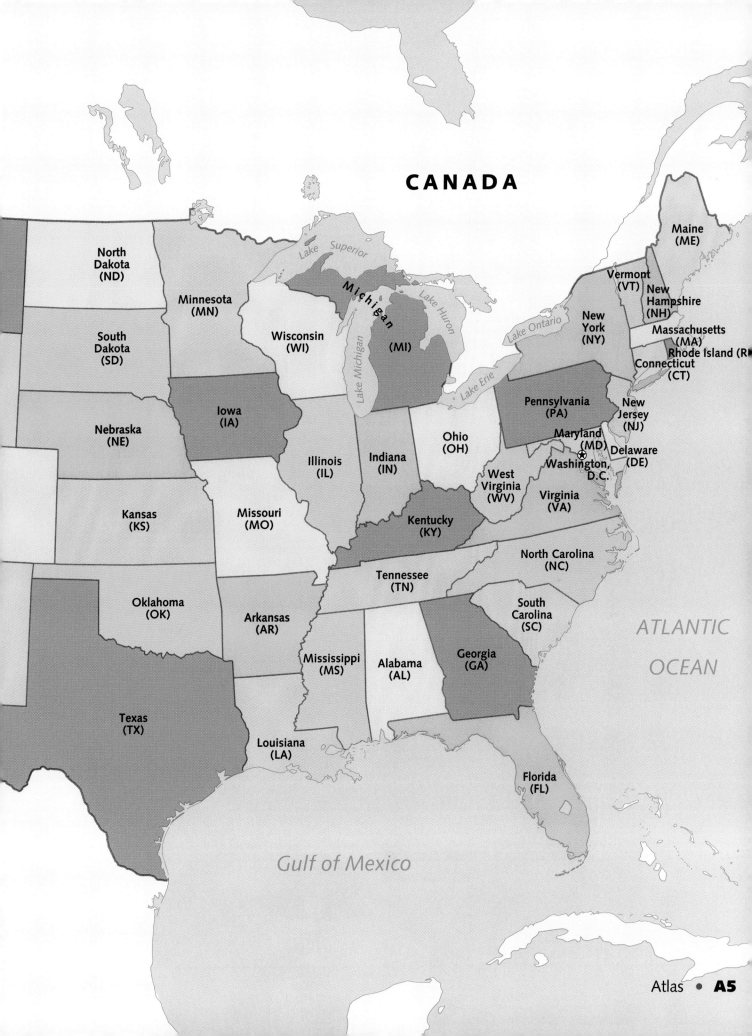

CANADA

Lake Superior

Michigan

Lake Huron

Lake Michigan

Lake Ontario

Lake Erie

North Dakota (ND)

Minnesota (MN)

South Dakota (SD)

Wisconsin (WI)

Michigan (MI)

Maine (ME)

Vermont (VT)

New Hampshire (NH)

New York (NY)

Massachusetts (MA)

Rhode Island (R

Connecticut (CT)

Nebraska (NE)

Iowa (IA)

Illinois (IL)

Indiana (IN)

Ohio (OH)

Pennsylvania (PA)

New Jersey (NJ)

Maryland (MD)

Delaware (DE)

Washington, D.C.

West Virginia (WV)

Virginia (VA)

Kansas (KS)

Missouri (MO)

Kentucky (KY)

North Carolina (NC)

Oklahoma (OK)

Arkansas (AR)

Tennessee (TN)

South Carolina (SC)

Mississippi (MS)

Alabama (AL)

Georgia (GA)

ATLANTIC OCEAN

Texas (TX)

Louisiana (LA)

Florida (FL)

Gulf of Mexico

UNIT 1

School Days

VOCABULARY

school

teacher

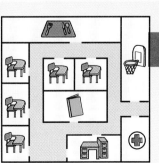

map

group

rule

Good Books, Good Times!

by Lee Bennett Hopkins

Good books.

Good times.

Good stories.

Good rhymes.

Good beginnings.

Good ends.

Good people.

Good friends.

Good fiction.

Good facts.

Good adventures.

Good acts.

Good stories.

Good rhymes.

Good books.

Good times.

My Classroom

I write in my classroom.

Dear Grandpa,
Here is my school.
This is my teacher.
These are my friends.
Love,
Megan

What would your letter say?

LESSON

1. title

Things I Learn

I learn how to read. To **learn** is to find out something new.

2. new word

I learn about
children far away.

3. picture

I learn to show how I feel.

4. story

How do pictures
and words help
you learn?

7

HOW TO

Learn from a Picture and a Map

1. Look at the picture of a classroom.

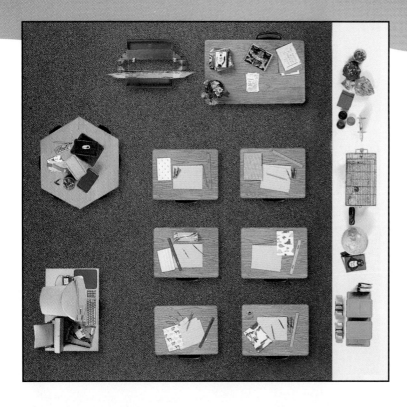

2. Look at a picture of the same classroom from above.

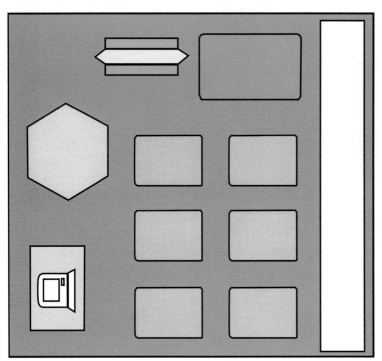

3. Look at a map of the classroom.

A **map** is a drawing. It shows what a place looks like from above.

Think and Do

Make a list of what you see on the map.

School Workers

We all work at school.

principal

custodian

teacher

servers

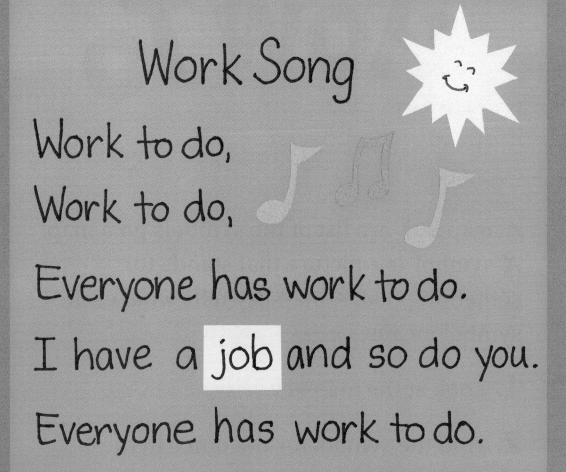

Work Song

Work to do,
Work to do,
Everyone has work to do.
I have a job and so do you.
Everyone has work to do.

What is your job at school?

How To

Read a Map Key

A **map key** is a list of the symbols on a map. A **symbol** is a picture that stands for something real. A map key tells what each symbol means.

1. Look at the map key.

2. Find the symbol for the office in the map key.

3. Where is the office on the map?

Think and Do

Tell how you would go from the office to the cafeteria.

School Map

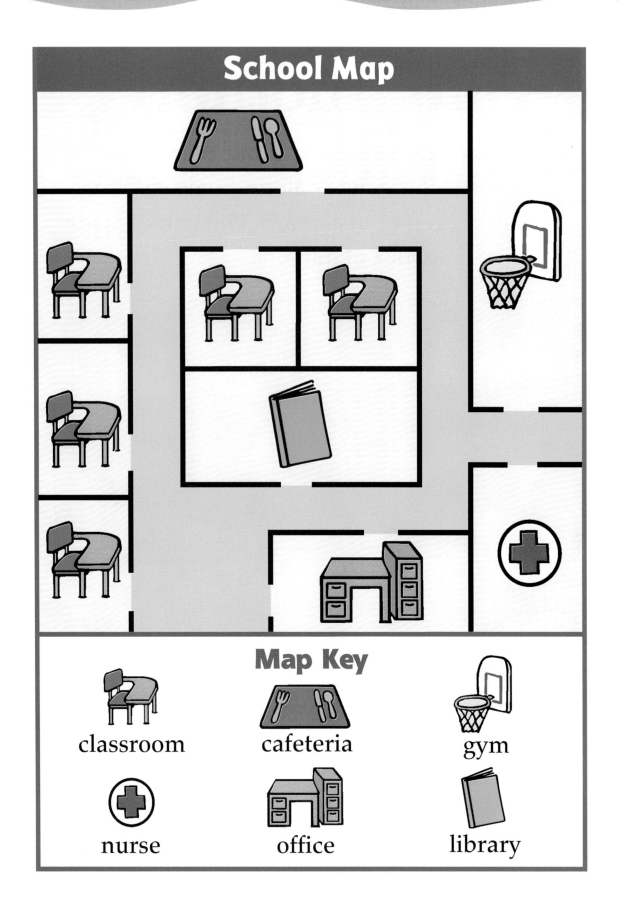

Map Key

classroom

cafeteria

gym

nurse

office

library

13

We Help One Another

We all have jobs to do in our classroom. Some children work alone. Some children work together in a **group**. One group made this scrapbook of our jobs.

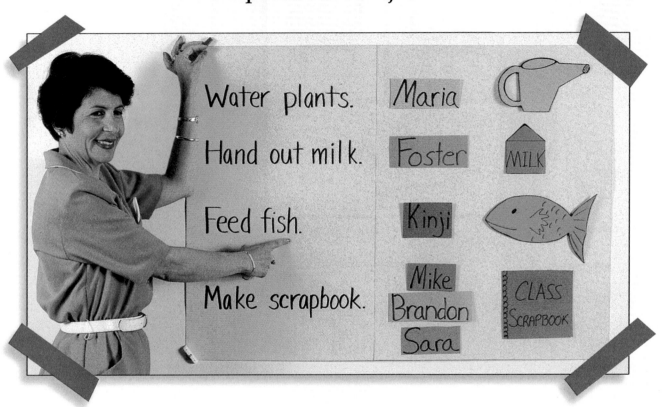

Water plants.   Maria

Hand out milk.   Foster   MILK

Feed fish.   Kinji

Make scrapbook.   Mike
                   Brandon   CLASS
                   Sara   SCRAPBOOK

What jobs would you show in your scrapbook?

Brainstorm

Joey is new in school.
What is happening?

How does Joey feel?
What would you do?

We Follow School Rules

A **rule** tells us what we should or should not do. Read this class list.

Class Rules

Stand in line.

Raise your hand.

Be quiet in the library.

Don't chew gum.

Look at the pictures. Who is following a rule? Who is not?

What rules would you add to the list?

Story Cloth

Look at the pictures. They will help you remember what you learned.

Talk About the Main Ideas

1. Children learn many new things in their classrooms.
2. School workers and children have important jobs at school.
3. Working together helps to get jobs done.
4. Following rules is an important part of learning to get along.

Tell a Story Pick one of the rooms in this school. Make up a story about the people in the room and what they are doing. Tell your story to the class.

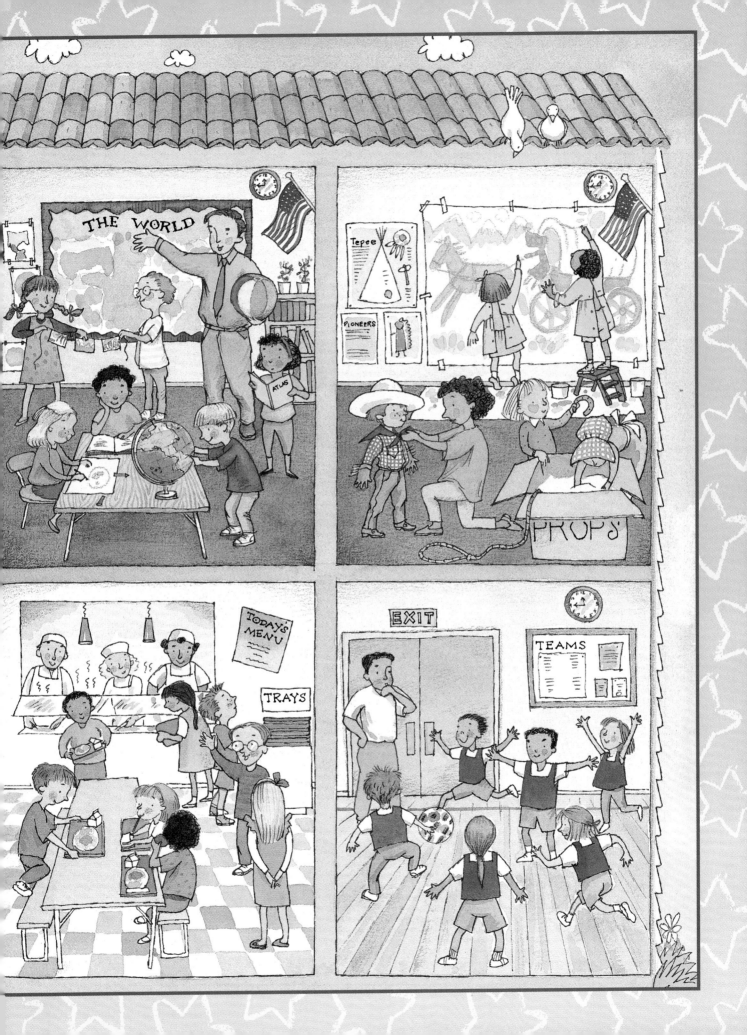

Review

Use Vocabulary

Which word goes with each picture?

teacher   **school**   **group**   **map**   **rule**

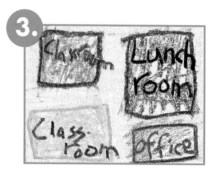

Check Understanding

1. Tell one thing you learn in the classroom.
2. Name two school workers and tell what they do.
3. What is your job as a school worker?
4. Why is working in a group important?

Think Critically

How do rules help you get along with others?

Apply Skills

How to Read a Map Key

The map shows a playground. Use the map and map key to answer the questions.

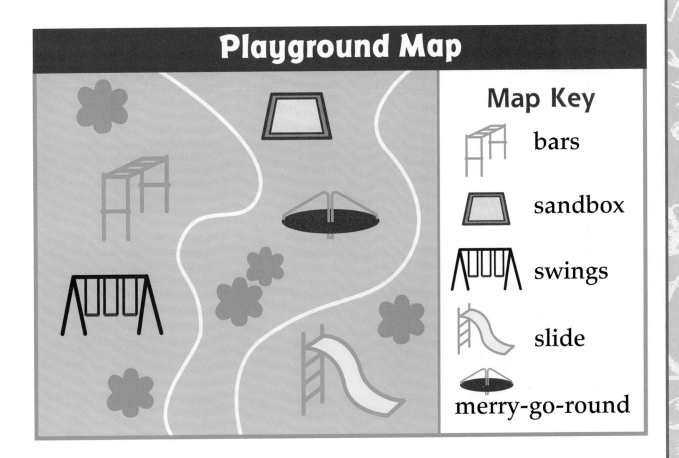

1. What can you learn from the map key?
2. What is between the sandbox and the slide?
3. What is closest to the swings?

Read More About It

Cleversticks by Bernard Ashley. Crown. A little boy is unhappy in school until everyone learns that he can do something very special.

At Home with My Family

VOCABULARY

family

change

money

choice

holiday

25

Home!
You're Where
It's Warm Inside

by Jack Prelutsky

Home! You are a special place;

you're where I wake and wash my face,

brush my teeth and comb my hair,

change my socks and underwear,

clean my ears and blow my nose,

try on all my parents' clothes.

Home! You're where it's warm inside,
where my tears are gently dried,
where I'm comforted and fed,
where I'm forced to go to bed,
where there's always love to spare;
Home! I'm glad that you are there.

Welcome Home

I live in a group. It is my **family**. Families have **needs**. A home is one of our needs. I wrote this story about homes.

My Family

A nest is a home for a bird.

A doghouse is a home for Rusty.

RUSTY

A house is a home
for some people.
An **apartment** is a
home for me.

What else do
families need?
Draw your
family at home.

HOW TO

Find a Home Address on a Map

Families have addresses. An **address** tells where people live. It has a number and a street name.

1. Look at the map on page 31. What is the number of the blue house?

2. What is the name of the street?

ELM ST.

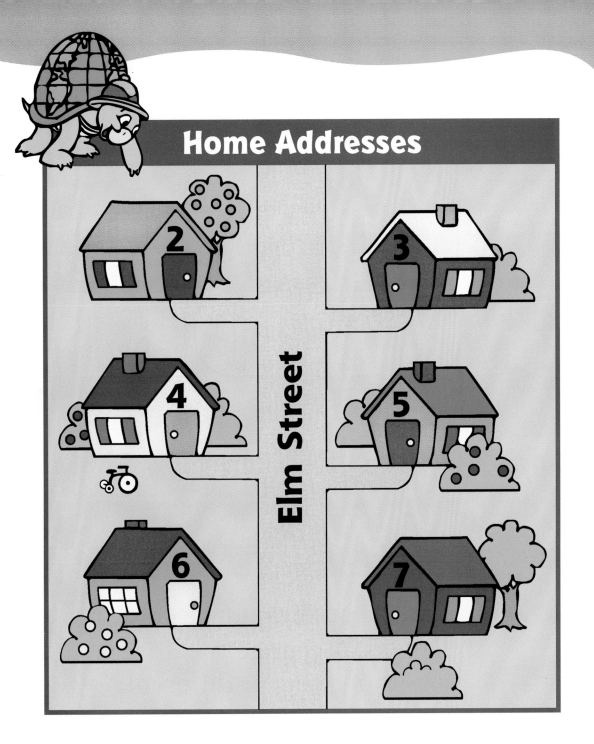

Home Addresses

Elm Street

Think and Do

Point to the green house on the map. What is the address?

LESSON

FLOWER GARDEN

EVE BUNTING

ILLUSTRATED BY KATHRYN HEWITT

Families go through
changes. A **change** is
something new or different.
Read how a girl made a
change to her home.

Garden in a shopping cart,
Doesn't it look great?
Garden on the checkout stand
I can hardly wait.

33

Garden in a cardboard box
Walking to the bus
Garden sitting on our laps
People smile at us!

Garden going up the stairs
Stopping at each floor
This garden's getting heavier!
At last—our own front door.

Hurry! Hurry! Get the trowel
Spread the papers thick.
Get the bag of potting soil
Get the planting mix.

36

Put purple pansies at each end
Daisies, white as snow
Daffodils, geraniums
and tulips in a row.

Garden in a window box
High above the street
Where butterflies
can stop and rest
And ladybugs can meet.

Walkers walking down below
Will lift their heads and see
Purple, yellow, red, and white
A color jamboree.

40

Candles on a birthday cake
Chocolate ice cream, too.
Happy, happy birthday, Mom!
A garden box—for you.

How did Mom's life change?

How To
Read a Time Line

In <u>Flower Garden</u>, you read about a birthday and a garden box. These were changes in a family. You can show changes on a time line. A **time line** shows when things happen. Look at Anna's time line.

1. What happens first on the time line?

2. What happens next?

3. What happens last?

Anna's Time Line

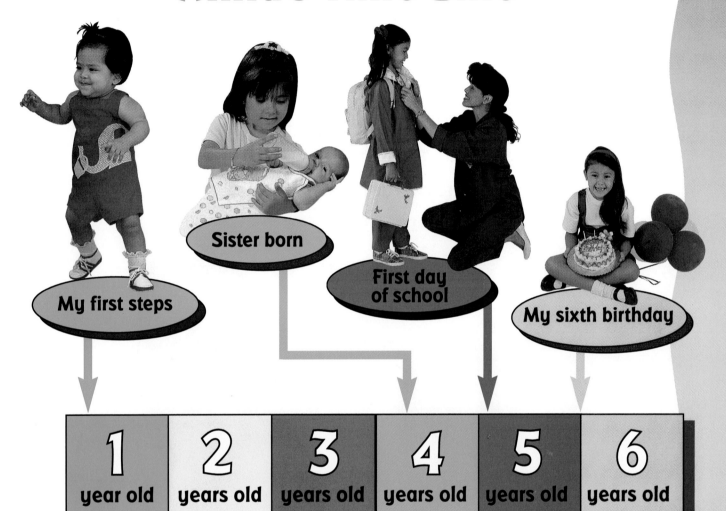

Sister born

My first steps

First day
of school

My sixth birthday

1	2	3	4	5	6
year old	years old	years old	years old	years old	years old

Think and Do

Anna lost her first tooth
just before her sixth birthday.
Where would the picture go
on the time line?

Families Make Choices

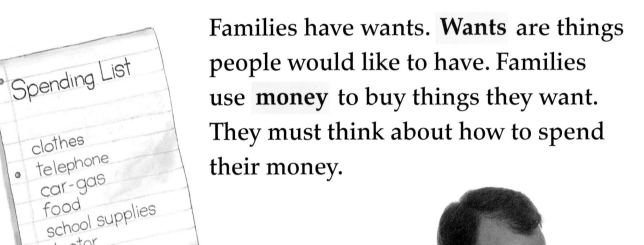

Spending List

- clothes
- telephone
- car-gas
- food
- school supplies
- doctor

Families have wants. **Wants** are things people would like to have. Families use **money** to buy things they want. They must think about how to spend their money.

I help my family shop.
What we pick to buy is a **choice**.
I have three brothers and sisters.
Which box of cereal is the
better choice?

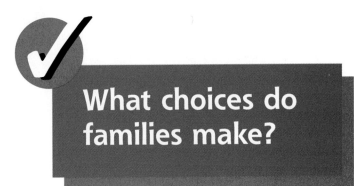

What choices do
families make?

How To

Make a Choice

Families cannot buy everything they want. They have to make choices. The Jones family is thinking about how to spend their money wisely.

1. What does the family want?

2. What questions do they need to ask?

3. What choice do you think the family made?

Think and Do

Think of three things you want. Tell how you would make a choice.

LESSON

Families Long Ago: A Thanksgiving Story

Long ago only American Indians lived on this land. They built their homes and farmed the land.

Then people from far away began to come to America. The Pilgrims wanted a new place to live.

They built homes and a village. American Indians showed the Pilgrims how to grow corn.

The Pilgrim families worked hard.
Pilgrim children helped.
Their plants grew, and they had a lot of food.

The Pilgrims invited the American Indians to share their meal. They thanked God for all their food.

Today we remember the Pilgrims and the Indians on a **holiday** called Thanksgiving Day.

How does your family celebrate Thanksgiving?

Trevor's Campaign for the Homeless

Hello, my name is Trevor. I live in Philadelphia. When I was eleven, I saw something bad on TV. I saw people living on the street because they had no homes.

I asked my parents to take me downtown that night. I gave my blanket and pillow to the first homeless person I met.

After that, my family and friends and other people helped. We started Trevor's Campaign for the Homeless. Trevor's Campaign is still helping homeless people.

One person can make a difference.

What Can You Do?

- Collect food and blankets for the homeless.
- Donate your old toys and clothes to a homeless shelter.

Story Cloth

Look at the pictures. They will help you remember what you learned.

Talk About the Main Ideas

1. Our families help us to meet our needs.
2. Families grow and change.
3. Families make choices about how to spend their money wisely.
4. Families long ago depended on each other, too.

Think Ahead What will a family be like 100 years from now? Draw how you think the family might be different from yours.

Now

Then

Review

Use Vocabulary

Pat made a picture about one of these words.

money

choice

family

change

holiday

1. Which word is Pat's picture about?
2. Choose a different word. Make a picture about it.

Check Understanding

1. What are two things all families need?
2. How does a move make a change in a family?
3. Why must families make choices about money?
4. Tell about a holiday your family likes.

Think Critically

How do people in a family show that they care about one another?

Apply Skills

How to Read a Time Line

Use the time line to answer these questions.

Birthday Time Line

Dad's birthday

Mom's birthday

Brother's birthday

| January | February | March |

1. Whose birthday comes first?

2. In what month is Mom's birthday?

3. Does brother's birthday come before or after Mom's?

Read More About It

It Takes a Village by Jane Cowen-Fletcher. Scholastic. Yemi's little brother wanders off, and she can't find him. Soon Yemi learns why her neighbors always say, "It takes a village to raise a child."

Living in a Community

VOCABULARY

city

neighborhood

services

leader

goods

59

I Live in a City

by Malvina Reynolds

I live in a city, yes I do,
I live in a city, yes I do,
I live in a city, yes I do,
Made by human hands.

Verse:
Black hands, white hands, yellow and brown,
All together built this town.
Black hands, white hands, yellow and brown,
All together make the wheels go 'round.

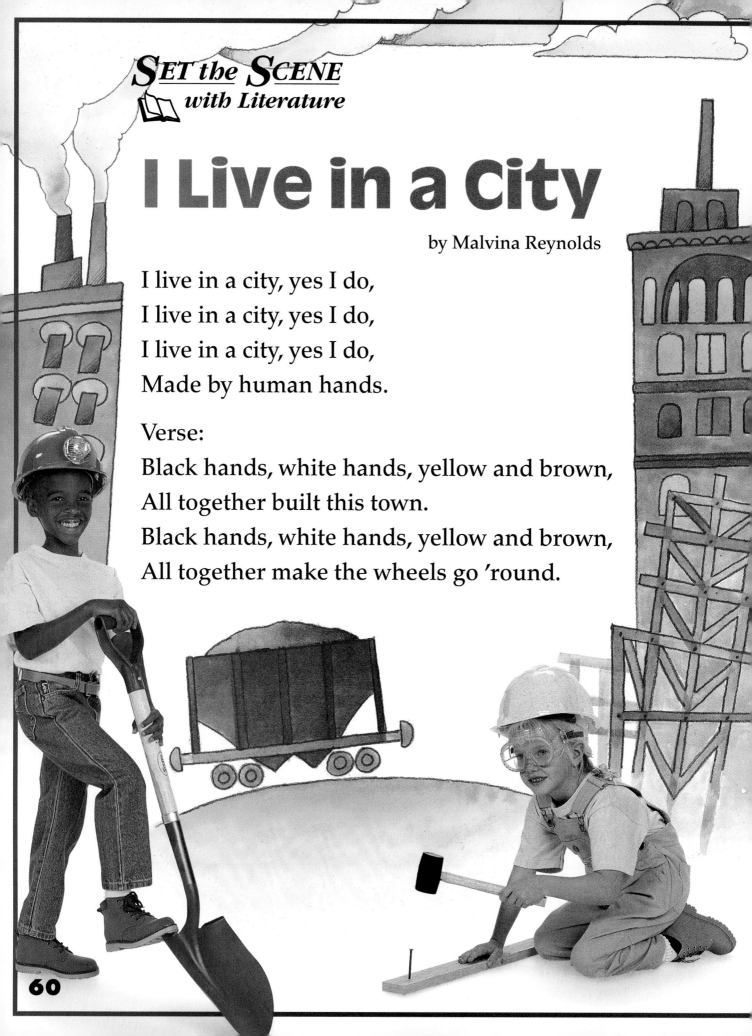

Brown hands, yellow hands, white and black,
Mined the coal and built the stack.
Brown hands, yellow hands, white and black,
Built the engine and laid the track.

Black hands, white hands, brown and tan,
Milled the flour and cleaned the pan.
Black hands, white hands, brown and tan,
The working woman and the working man.

Meet My Neighbors

A place where people live is a **community**. A **city** is a large community. A city has many **neighborhoods**. Read about the people who live in a city and its neighborhoods.

Hello, I'm Lisa. Welcome to my community. Come and meet some neighbors.

Miss Tims delivers our mail.

We buy bread from
Mr. Ross.

Nikki is a tennis teacher. People in the city play many sports.

My mom works at the museum. You can see things from all over the world at the museum. I learned how to make things out of clay at the museum.

Mr. Loomis takes care of our park. We like to ride our bikes in the park.

Officer Bob and Officer Dan help keep our neighborhood safe.

Who do you know in your community?

Community Leaders

Julio is talking to people about services. **Services** are jobs people do for others. Julio asked the mayor of Laredo, Texas, about his service job.

Julio: What does a mayor do?

Mayor Ramírez: I am a community **leader**.
My job is to serve the people of our city.
I meet with other leaders of the city.
We help run the community.

BLAS CASTANEDA   SAUL N. RAMIREZ, JR., Mayor   CECILIA MAY MORENO MAYOR PRO TEM

Julio: Where do you work?

Mayor Ramírez: My office is in City Hall.

Julio: Why do you like being a mayor?

Mayor Ramírez: I like helping the people of our city.

Who are the leaders in your community?

67

How To

Find Directions on a Map

Maps can show where places are in a community. We use four **directions** to find places on a map. They are north, south, east, and west.

1. Find the north arrow on the map. Move your finger in the direction of the north arrow. You are going north.

2. Find Main Street. Move your finger from First Street to Third Street on Main Street. You are going south.

3. Find east and west on the map.

Tiny Town

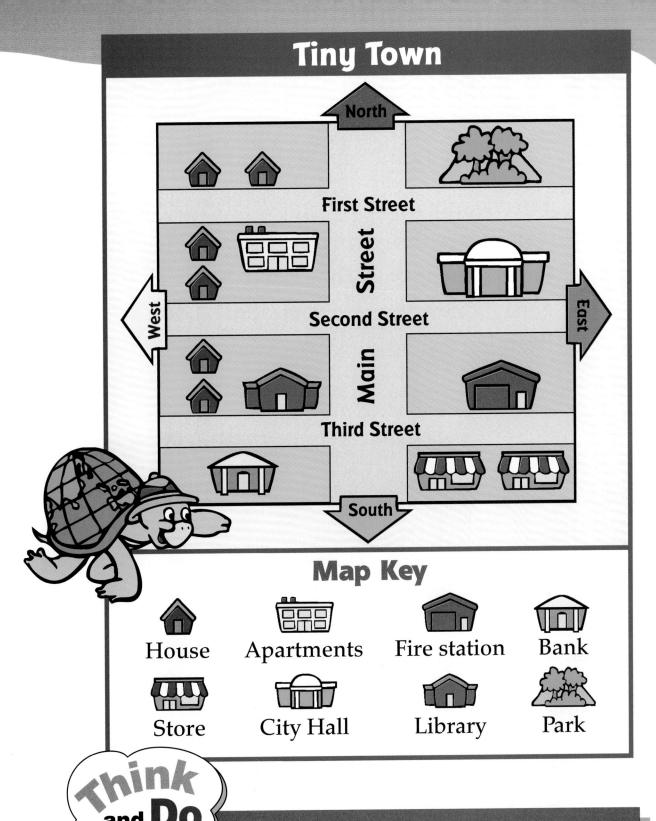

Map Key

House Apartments Fire station Bank

Store City Hall Library Park

Think and Do

The library is on fire. In which direction will the firefighters go to get from the fire station to the fire?

Trading Goods and Services

We use money to buy goods and services. **Goods** are things people use. People work to earn the money they need. Some children earn money doing jobs at home. Look at Brandon's shopping list.

My Shopping List

color markers
baseball bat
Get bike fixed.
paints
dog leash
dog food

What service is being done in this shop?

What goods can be found in these stores?

How do you spend your money?

71

SKILLS
HOW TO
Read a Table

A **table** lists things in groups. This table shows who sells goods and who gives services.

1. Which side of the table shows people who sell goods? Which side shows people who give services?

2. Find the bus driver. Does the bus driver sell goods or give a service?

3. Who sells goods that people eat?

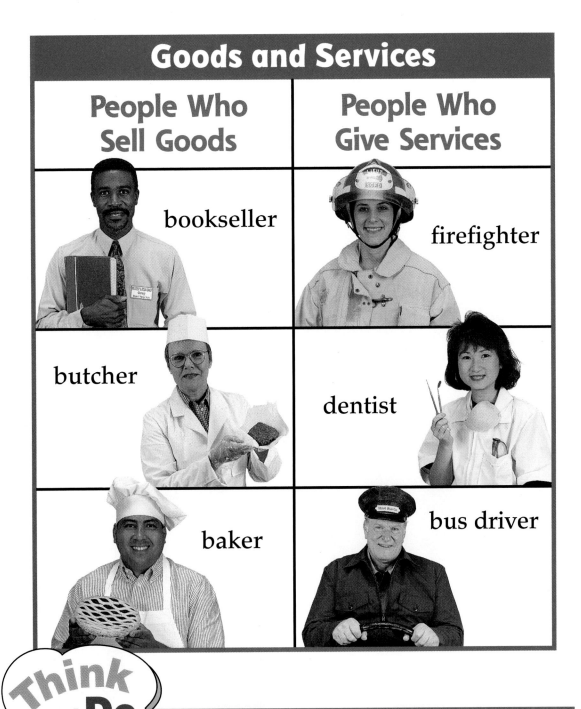

Goods and Services

People Who Sell Goods	People Who Give Services
bookseller	firefighter
butcher	dentist
baker	bus driver

Think and Do

Add two people to this table. Who would you add to the goods list? Who would you add to the services list?

Getting from Here to There

There are many ways to move from place to place. The ways people and goods travel change over time.

People and goods travel on land.

UNITED STATES POSTAGE
3¢ Charter

THE BALTIMORE & OHIO RAILROAD CHARTERED FEB. 28, 1827
125 YEARS OF RAIL TRANSPORTATION

People and goods travel on water.

People and goods travel in the air.

How does travel bring people together?

Kids Against Crime

Hello, my name is Linda. I live in San Bernardino, California. When I was twelve, I started a group called Kids Against Crime. This group teaches children how to be safe from crime.

Kids Against Crime puts on plays and fairs at schools. We also fingerprint children in the community. So far, we have fingerprinted thousands of girls and boys!

78

We started a telephone Help Hotline for children. Now children who are lonely or scared can call someone. Children run Kids Against Crime. But both children and adults volunteer to work there.

What Can You Do?

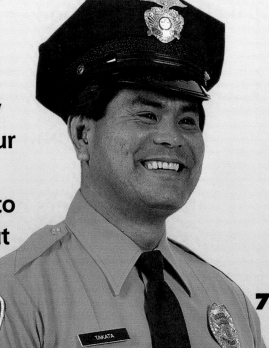

- **Write to Kids Against Crime to find out how to help children in your community.**

- **Invite a police officer to your class to talk about how to stay safe from crime.**

Story Cloth

Look at the picture. It will help you remember what you learned.

Talk About the Main Ideas

1. Different people and groups make up a community.
2. Community leaders help people get along.
3. People in a community depend on each other for goods and services.
4. People and goods move in many different ways.

Solve a Problem What is a problem this community might have? Tell how community leaders might help solve the problem.

Review

Use Vocabulary

Which word does not belong in each row? Tell why.

1. **leader**   mayor, dancer, principal

2. **goods**   food, clothes, rain

3. **services**   fight fires, make cars, cut hair

4. **city**   barns, stores, homes

5. **neighborhood**   houses, schools, whales

Check Understanding

1. How are all communities the same?
2. Name two service workers.
   Tell what each does.
3. What do people trade to get goods and services?
4. How do people and goods travel?

Think Critically

Why do people in a community need leaders?

Apply Skills

How to Find Directions on a Map

Use the map to find places in the community.

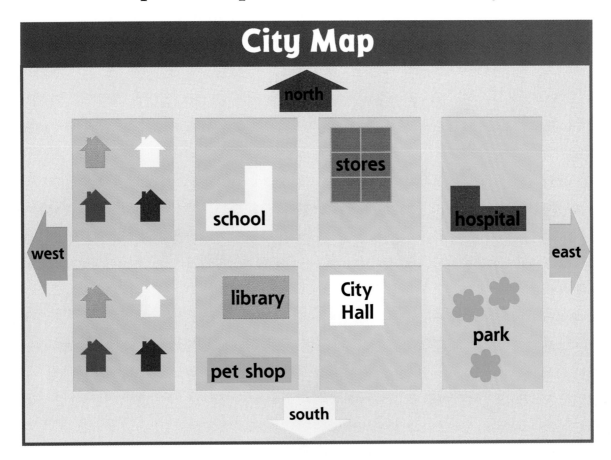

1. What is north of City Hall?
2. What building is on the east side of town?
3. In what direction would you go to get from the hospital to the school?

Read More About It

The Big Green Pocketbook by Candice Ransom. HarperCollins. A little girl fills her pocketbook with interesting things from a trip around town.

In and Around the Land

VOCABULARY

resource

farm

84

factory

recycle

85

From the Yard of My House

by F. Isabel Campoy

From the yard of my house I see my street.
From the end of the street I see my city.
From the top of the tower I see the valley,
and you?
What can you see from the end of your alley?

"I see cars passing by,
motorcycles,
bicycles,
and trucks.
They come from faraway places
carrying goods from many lands."

From the top of the tower I see the valley,
and you?
What can you see from the end of your alley?

Land and Water

mountain

river

lake

hill

plain

ocean

This drawing shows different kinds of land
and different kinds of water. Read the picture
dictionary to find out about each one.

hill

A **hill** is land that rises up high but not as high as a mountain.

lake

A **lake** is a body of water that has land around it.

mountain

A **mountain** is the highest kind of land.

ocean

An **ocean** is the largest body of water, and its water is salty.

plain

A **plain** is land that is mostly flat.

river

A **river** is a long body of water that flows through the land.

What kinds of land and water are near your community?

SKILLS
How To
Find Land and Water on a Map

This map shows land and water. It uses pictures and colors to show where things are.

1. Look at the map key. What pictures and colors do you see?

2. Find the river and the lake. How are they the same?

Think and Do

Look at the map. What is between the mountains and the hiking trail?

90

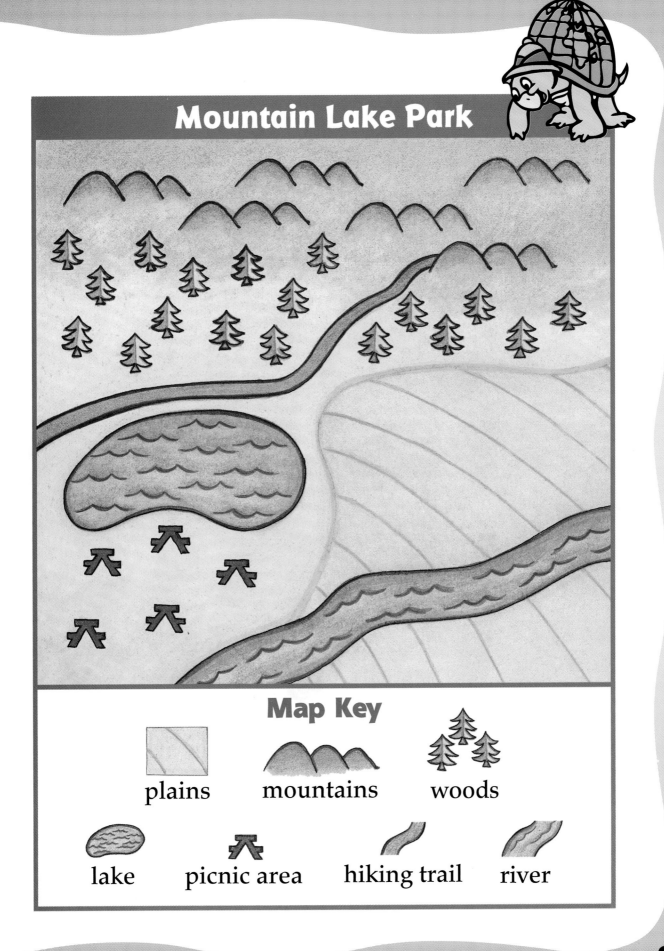

Mountain Lake Park

Map Key

plains   mountains   woods

lake   picnic area   hiking trail   river

Our Treasured Resources

A **resource** is something people use to meet their needs. Trees, soil, water, oil, and gas are resources. Where do these resources come from? Read this report to find out.

Trees are an important resource. Many trees grow in a **forest**. Wood and food come from trees. Wood is used to make buildings and furniture. Apples and walnuts are two foods that grow on trees.

Did you know that paper is made from wood?

Oil and gas are resources. They come from under the ground. People use oil and gas to heat their homes and cook their food. Some oil is made into gasoline. Oil and gasoline help run cars.

Soil is another resource. Soil is the ground
that is needed for trees and other plants
to grow.

Soil is very important to farms. A **farm**
is land that is used to grow plants for
food and clothing. Farmers grow plants
and raise animals to meet our needs.

Water is a resource, too. People cannot live without water. Water comes from lakes, rivers, and oceans.

Water is important for drinking. Most drinking water comes from lakes and rivers. Water also gives us food. Fish come from lakes, rivers, and oceans.

What resources do you use every day?

The Cheese Factory

Do you know what resources are used to make cheese? Mrs. Karl's class visited a factory to find out. A **factory** is a place where something is made.

Cheese

We like it on sandwiches, tacos, and crackers.

We spread it and slice it and grate it.

There's nothing quite like it for after-school snackers.

Oh dear. It's all gone. Guess I ate it!

This is the way cheese begins. First, dairy farmers raise the cows that give us milk.

Next, trucks take milk from the dairy farm to the cheese factory. There the milk is made into cheese.

To make the cheese, the milk is heated
and cooled. Then the liquid part is
drained away. The solid part is pressed
into blocks.

The blocks are salted and dipped in wax. When the cheese is ready, it is cut into small pieces. Finally, trucks carry the cheese to stores.

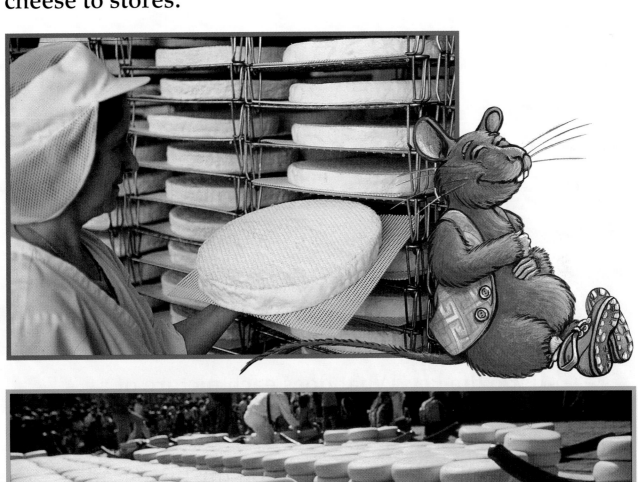

✓ **What surprised you about how cheese is made?**

How To

Read a Pictograph

After the field trip, Mrs. Karl's class made a pictograph. A **pictograph** uses pictures to show how many there are of something.

1. What is the title of this pictograph?

2. Find the key. What does each picture of a face stand for?

3. Find and name the foods on the pictograph.

4. Find the milk. How many faces are across from the milk? How many children had milk?

Dairy Foods We Ate at Lunch

milk	
ice cream	
cheese	
yogurt	
butter	

Key
 = 1 child

What dairy food did the most children eat?

Mr. Smith's class made a flyer about saving resources.

How To

Reduce

Reuse

Recycle

JUICE

Reduce

- Turn off the water while you brush your teeth.

- Walk or ride your bike instead of having someone drive you.

- Shut off the lights when you leave the room. That saves electricity.

Reuse

You can reuse many things.

- Try reusing plastic bags and glass bottles.

- Make a pencil holder from a can.

- Grow plants in a plastic bottle.

Recycle

- Used plastic, paper, glass, and cans can be recycled.

- Find a place to collect the things you can recycle.

- Leave them for pick-up or take them to a recycling center.

What things do you reduce, reuse, or recycle?

Brainstorm

What is happening?
Work with a friend.
How are the pictures different?

What would you do?
Write a rule.
Make a sign.

SKILLS

HOW TO

Find Out What People Think

A first-grade class is planning a picnic. The children cannot decide whether to take paper or plastic cups and plates. They decide to find out what everyone thinks.

1. How will they find out what the children think?

2. What are they asking?

3. How can they use what they find out?

Think and Do

How can the answers to the questions help you?

What Would You Take?

If you are planning a picnic, what would you take?

Circle one kind of plate and one kind of cup.

1. Plates: plastic   paper   other

   Reason _____

2. Cups: plastic   paper   other

   Reason _____

Story Cloth

Follow the pictures. They will help you remember what you learned.

Talk About the Main Ideas

1. There are different kinds of land and water.
2. Resources come from land and water.
3. Factories use resources to make things we need.
4. People help save resources.

Draw Me I am a resource that lives in a brook. If you want to catch me, you need a sharp hook. People cook me and serve me on a dish. Do you know what I am? I'm just a little _____! Think of your own resource riddle.

Review

Use Vocabulary

Which word goes with each box?

factory   **farm**   **resource**   **recycle**

1. something people use that comes from the Earth

2. place where people raise plants and animals for food

3. place where things are made that people want to buy

4. make something old into something new

Check Understanding

1. Name three kinds of land and tell about each.
2. Name two resources that come from the land. How do people use each of them?
3. How do people work together to save resources?
4. Why are farms and factories important?

Think Critically

How can saving the Earth's resources help us?

Apply Skills

How to Read a Pictograph

Use the pictograph to answer the questions.

Our Favorite Places To Go

Mountains	(7 figures)
Ocean	(9 figures)
Farm	(4 figures)
City	(2 figures)

1. Which place do most of the children like best?
2. How many children chose the mountains?
3. More children chose the farm than the city. How many more chose the farm?

Read More About It

<u>The Way to Captain Yankee's</u> by Anne Rockwell. Macmillan. Miss Calico gets lost on her way to visit Captain Yankee. A map helps her solve her problem.

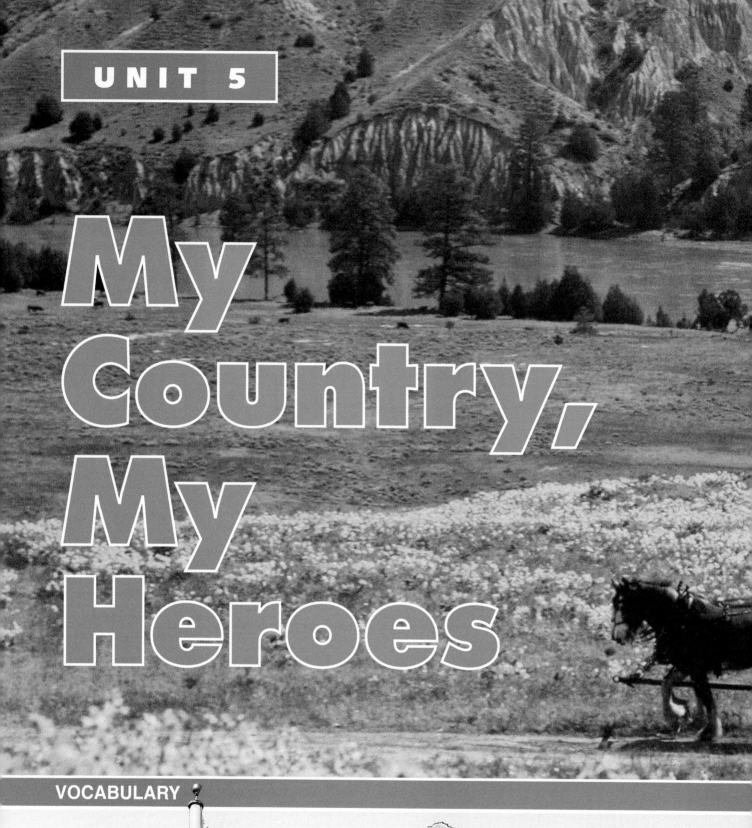

My Country, My Heroes

VOCABULARY

flag

country

state

President

law

DONT WALK

WALK

113

The Pledge of Allegiance

I pledge allegiance
to the **flag** of the United
States of America, and to the
Republic for which it stands,
one Nation under God,
indivisible, with liberty
and justice for all.

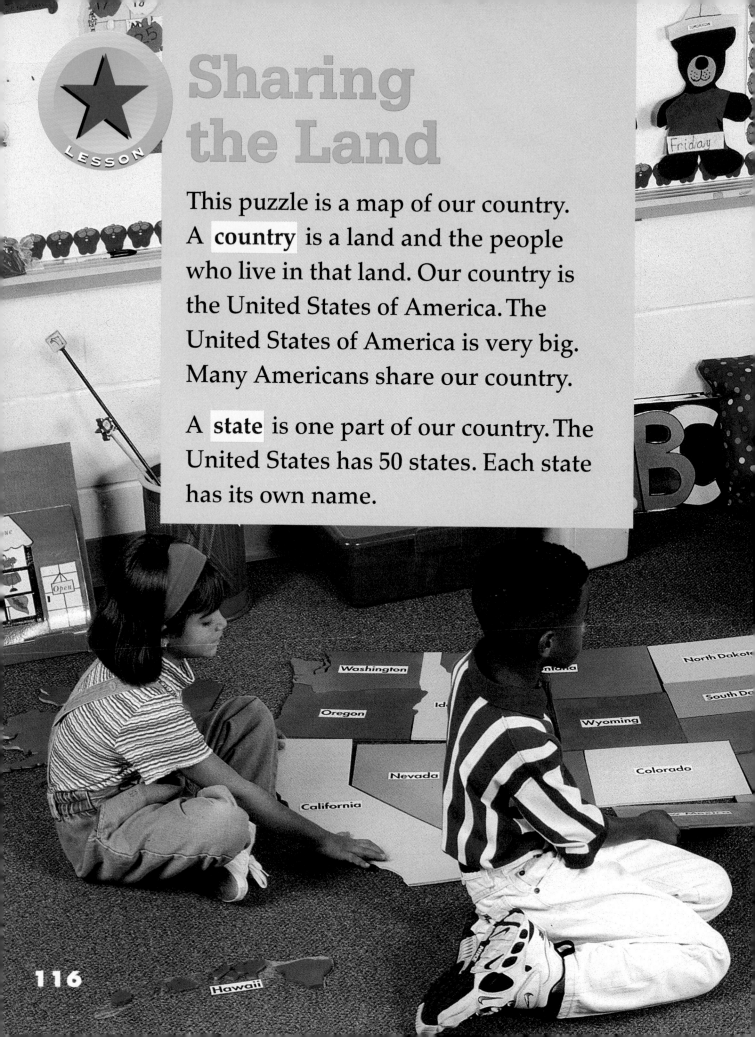

Sharing the Land

This puzzle is a map of our country. A **country** is a land and the people who live in that land. Our country is the United States of America. The United States of America is very big. Many Americans share our country.

A **state** is one part of our country. The United States has 50 states. Each state has its own name.

United States of America

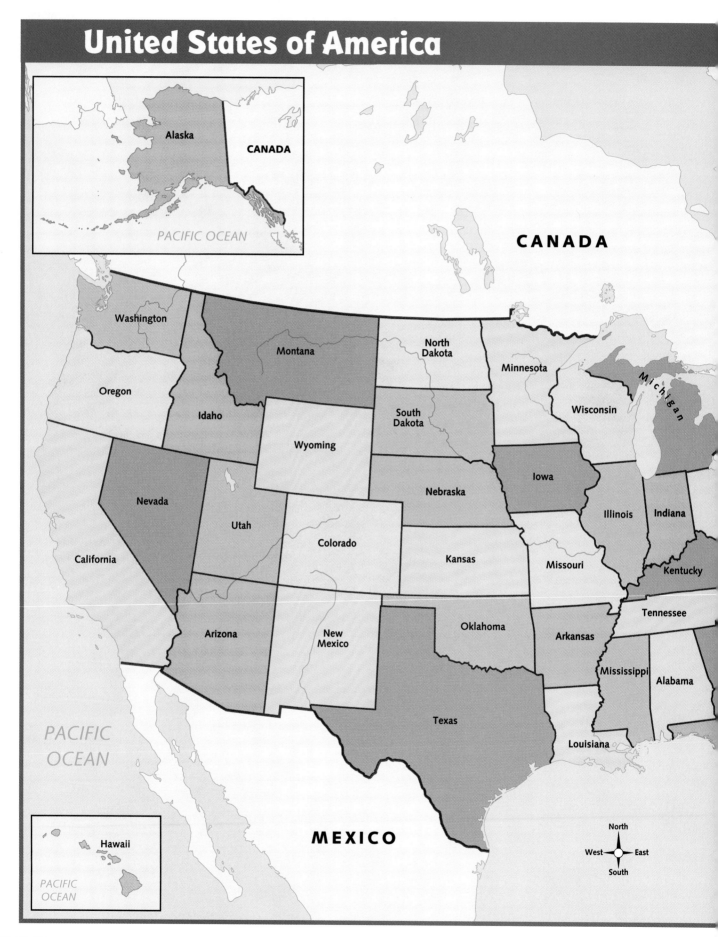

Alaska

CANADA

PACIFIC OCEAN

CANADA

Washington

Montana

North Dakota

Minnesota

Michigan

Oregon

Idaho

South Dakota

Wisconsin

Wyoming

Iowa

Nevada

Utah

Nebraska

Illinois

Indiana

California

Colorado

Kansas

Missouri

Kentucky

Tennessee

Arizona

New Mexico

Oklahoma

Arkansas

Mississippi

Alabama

Texas

Louisiana

PACIFIC OCEAN

Hawaii

PACIFIC OCEAN

MEXICO

North

West   East

South

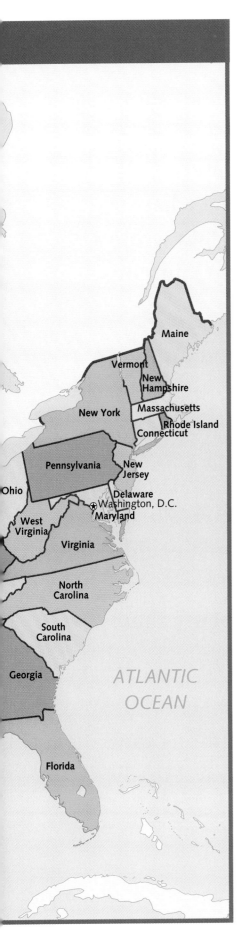

This is another map of our country. It shows the countries that are our neighbors. Mexico is our neighbor to the south. Canada is our neighbor to the north.

This map also shows two oceans. The Atlantic Ocean is east of our country. The Pacific Ocean is to the west.

In which state do you live? Which states are your neighbors?

119

LESSON

Two Peoples Meet

This is the story of how two different peoples first met long, long ago. We know what happened because a ship's captain wrote a log. His name was Christopher Columbus. Read about his ocean voyage.

Friday, August 3, 1492. Columbus and his men sailed away from Spain. They sailed on three ships called the *Niña*, the *Pinta*, and the *Santa Maria*.

Sunday, September 9, 1492. Columbus and his men could no longer see land. They were afraid they would not see their homes for a long time.

Thursday, October 11, 1492, late at night. Columbus saw light from far away. Finally, Columbus was near land.

120

Friday, October 12, 1492. Columbus and his men landed on the beach of an island. Soon they met friendly people who lived on that island and on others nearby.

North America

Spain

San Salvador

Atlantic Ocean

Africa

Hispaniola

121

We call the people that Columbus met
American Indians. They had never
seen anyone like Columbus before.
The newcomers wore strange clothes.
They did not speak the same words.

Columbus and the Indians traded many
things. The Indians gave Columbus
foods that he had never tasted before.

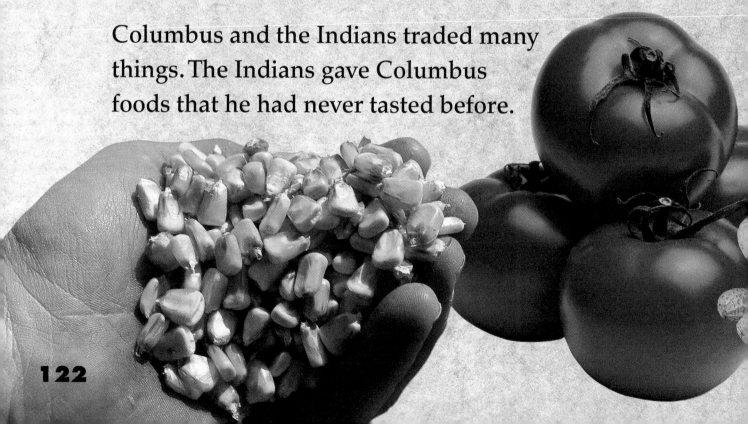

Columbus took corn, peanuts, sweet potatoes, and tomatoes back to Spain.

One year later he returned and brought the Indians horses, pigs, goats, and sheep.

Columbus told many people about the islands he found. After a while many people followed Columbus across the ocean. Life changed forever for everyone.

Why do you think people today celebrate Columbus Day?

Independence Day

LESSON

Our favorite holiday is the Fourth
of July. It is called Independence Day.
That is our country's birthday.

My Favorite Holiday

Long ago, America belonged to a country called England. Americans wanted to rule themselves.

On July 4, 1776, American leaders signed the Declaration of Independence. It told the King of England that Americans wanted to be free.

Americans fought to be free. General
George Washington led the Americans
against English soldiers. He helped
the Americans win a hard war.

Washington was a **hero**. Americans chose him as the first President of the United States of America.

The **President** is the leader of our country. His wife was Martha Washington, our country's first First Lady.

What other heroes do you know?

SKILLS

HOW TO

Make a Choice by Voting

How do people become President or mayor? Americans choose their leaders by voting. A **vote** is a choice that gets counted. The one who gets the most votes wins. Here's how it works.

1. Imagine that Freetown needs an animal control officer. Some popular storybook animals want the job.

2. Only one can become the animal control officer. The people must choose by voting. The names are put on a ballot. Each person has only one vote. Who a person votes for is a secret.

3. After everyone votes, the votes are counted. The person with the most votes wins.

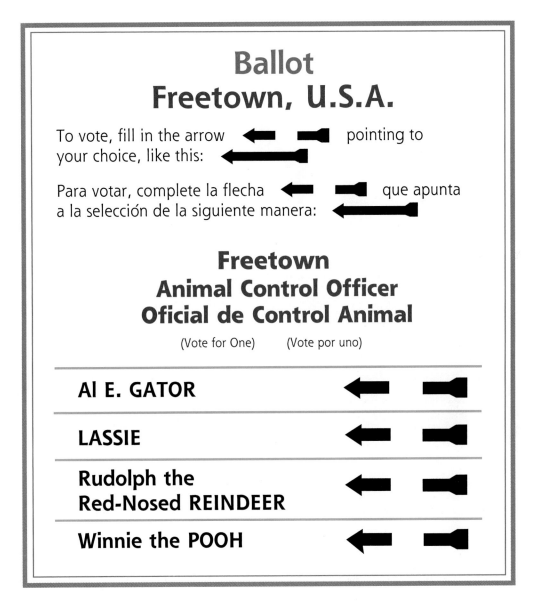

Ballot
Freetown, U.S.A.

To vote, fill in the arrow ⬅ ◼ pointing to your choice, like this: ⬅

Para votar, complete la flecha ⬅ ◼ que apunta a la selección de la siguiente manera: ⬅

Freetown
Animal Control Officer
Oficial de Control Animal

(Vote for One)   (Vote por uno)

Al E. GATOR   ⬅ ◼

LASSIE   ⬅ ◼

**Rudolph the
Red-Nosed REINDEER**   ⬅ ◼

Winnie the POOH   ⬅ ◼

Think and Do

Tell why voting is a good way to choose leaders.

Brainstorm

What is happening?
Work with a group.
Make a list of what you see.

What would you do?
Choose a way to show
the class your ideas.

LEARN
with
LITERATURE

Focus on pride in our country

AMERICA the BEAUTIFUL

Katharine Lee Bates

illustrated by **Neil Waldman**

O beautiful for spacious skies,

For amber waves of grain,

For purple mountain majesties
Above the fruited plain!

America! America!

God shed His grace on thee

And crown thy good
with brotherhood

138

From sea to shining sea!

✔

What do you think makes America beautiful?

How To

Read a Diagram

Miss Liberty is our country's most famous statue. This picture names the parts of the statue. It also shows you what it looks like inside. This kind of picture is called a **diagram**.

1. Name the parts of the Statue of Liberty.

2. Find Miss Liberty's crown. Did you know that people inside can look out through windows in the crown?

3. How can people get up to the crown?

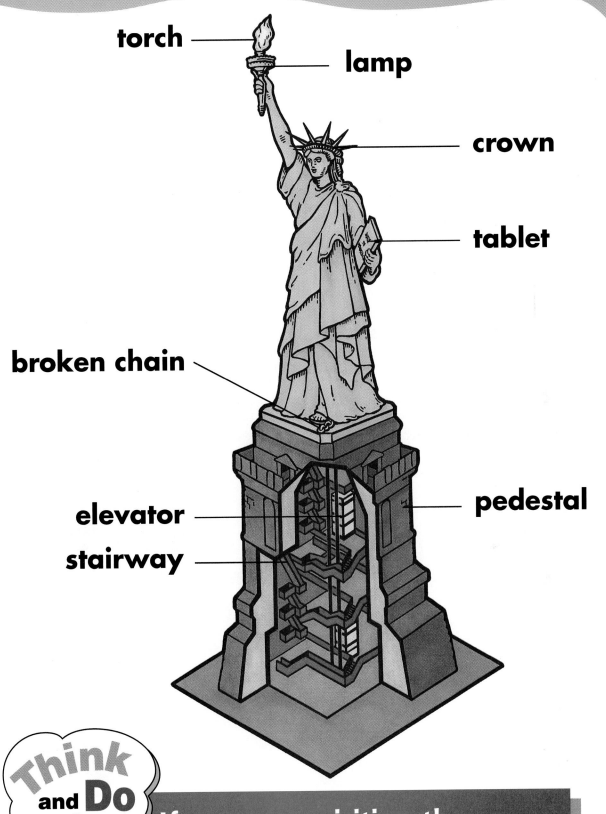

torch

lamp

crown

tablet

broken chain

pedestal

elevator

stairway

If you were visiting the Statue of Liberty, how could this diagram help you?

Story Cloth

Look at the pictures. They will help you remember what you learned.

Talk About the Main Ideas

1. The United States today has fifty states.
2. Long ago, Columbus led the way for new people to come to America.
3. Americans fought a war for freedom and our country was born.
4. Americans are proud of their free and beautiful country.

Act It Out   You and your friend are sailing to America. Tell why you want to make this country your new home.

Review

Use Vocabulary

Which word goes with each line?

state	**1.** United States, Mexico, Canada
country	**2.** Alaska, Ohio, Texas, Hawaii
law	**3.** fifty stars, thirteen stripes
President	**4.** Do not speed. Stop at red lights.
flag	**5.** leader, George Washington

Check Understanding

1. What is the difference between a country and a state?
2. What people were already living in America when Columbus landed there?
3. What foods did the Indians give Columbus? What did Columbus give the Indians?
4. In 1776 the Americans went to war with England. Why?

Think Critically

Why is voting important to Americans?

Apply Skills

How to Make a Choice by Voting

Mrs. Lee's class wanted a class president.
They wanted Jeff or Tamika for the job.
Each child in the class voted. The table
shows who won.

1. Who will be the class president? Why?
2. How many children voted for Jeff?
3. There are 20 children in the class. How many
   times did each child vote?

Read More About It

Buttons for General Washington by Peter and
Connie Roop. Carolrhoda. A young boy helps
the Americans in their fight against England.
Find out how his coat buttons helped General
Washington win the war.

My World Near and Far

VOCABULARY

world

globe

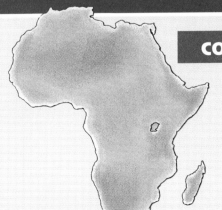

continent

language

Public Library

Biblioteca Pública

It's a Small World

by Richard M. Sherman and Robert B. Sherman

It's a world of laughter,
a world of tears,
It's a world of hopes
and a world of fears.
There's so much that we share,
and it's time we're aware,
It's a small world after all.

Mexico

148

It's a small world after all.

It's a small world after all.

It's a small world after all.

It's a small, small world.

There is just one moon
and one golden sun,
And a smile means friendship
to everyone.
Though the mountains divide
and the oceans are wide,
It's a small world after all.

149

Where in the World Do People Live?

My grandma traveled around the world. The **world** is all the people and places on the Earth. Today we searched through Grandma's trunk in the attic. She showed me the things she brought back from the places she visited and the people she met.

Grandma showed me a dress she bought in Mexico. I found a fan from Korea. Grandma brought dolls from Russia.

Grandma took pictures of wild elephants in Tanzania. She climbed to the top of the Acropolis in Greece.

Grandma made me feel like I'd been around the world, too.

How can you learn about the world?

SKILLS

How To

Use a Globe

You can find all the places in the world on a globe. A **globe** is a model of the Earth.

1. Look at the picture of the globe. How is it like the Earth?

2. Now look at the drawings on page 153. Each drawing shows half of the globe. You can see all the oceans and continents. A **continent** is a very large piece of land. North America is our continent. Find North America.

3. Now find the place that is farthest north on the globe.

152

The World

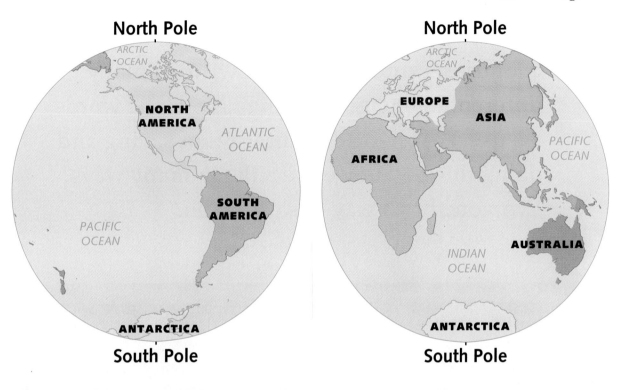

North Pole

ARCTIC OCEAN

NORTH AMERICA

ATLANTIC OCEAN

SOUTH AMERICA

PACIFIC OCEAN

ANTARCTICA

South Pole

North Pole

ARCTIC OCEAN

EUROPE

ASIA

AFRICA

PACIFIC OCEAN

AUSTRALIA

INDIAN OCEAN

ANTARCTICA

South Pole

That is the North Pole. The place that is farthest south is the South Pole. Is North America closer to the North Pole or the South Pole?

Think and Do

Name each continent. Name each ocean.

People Are People Everywhere

Our class is learning about children in other countries. People speak and write in many different languages. A **language** is the words we use. We have different ways of saying and doing things, but we are alike in many ways. Everyone has a way to say "Hello."

Hello! I live near a forest in Canada.

Jambo! I live on a farm in Somalia.

Salaam A'leikum! I live in Jordan.
My family has a pet goat.

¡Hola! My grandmother is teaching me to weave in Peru.

Bonjour! My friends and I enjoy going to a carnival in France.

Konnichewa! Japanese families like to play in the park.

How many ways can you say "hello"?

People Everywhere Are Linked

People all over the world trade with one another. People in other countries buy goods that are made in the United States. And people in the United States buy goods that are made in other countries.

This picture is from a magazine in Japan. It shows an American camera that people in Japan buy.

158

Mexico sells many beautiful things to people in the United States. People in the United States buy silver, jewels, and painted bowls from Mexico. Mexico also sells a lot of oil and food to the United States.

HOW TO

Use a Bar Graph

Spencer has toys and games made in different countries. He wanted to know how many came from each country. Spencer made a bar graph to show what he found. A **bar graph** helps you count how much or how many.

1. How many countries are shown on the bar graph?

2. Place your finger on the word <u>Thailand</u>. Count how many green boxes are next to <u>Thailand</u>. How many toys from Thailand does Spencer have?

3. From which country does Spencer have one toy?

Spencer's Toys

	0	1	2	3	4	5
United States						
Japan						
Denmark						
Thailand						

Think and Do

Which country made the greatest number of toys? Which country made the fewest?

We Share the Planet

There are ways people work together to solve problems on our planet. Our **planet** is the Earth. All kinds of animals share our planet with us. A special zoo in Texas works with people around the world to help save animals in danger.

My name is Emily and I love animals. I talked with Pat Burchfield last week. He works at the Gladys Porter Zoo. Here are some things I found out.

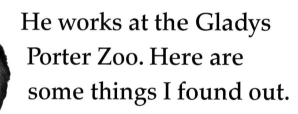

Emily: How many animals are in your zoo?

Mr. Burchfield: We have almost 400 different kinds of animals. They come from all over the world.

Emily: Why are some of these animals in danger?

Mr. Burchfield: Some people break the law by hunting animals that are in danger. Some people destroy animals' homes when they clear the land where animals live.

Emily: How do you help the animals?

Mr. Burchfield: We give them the food and the homes they need to live. We care for their young. Some animals are sick or hurt. We give them medicine and help them become healthy.

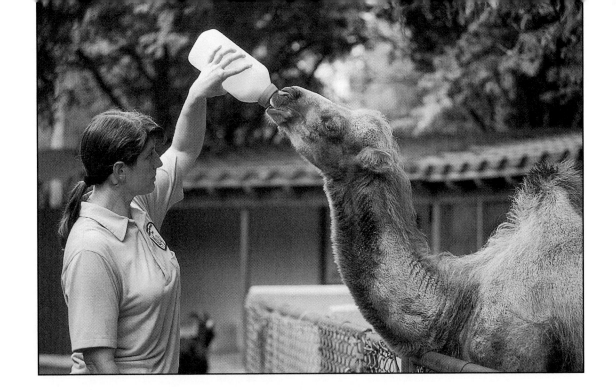

Emily: What will happen to these animals?

Mr. Burchfield: Some animals will always live here. We will raise other animals until they are well or until their homes are safe. Then we will send some back to live in the wild.

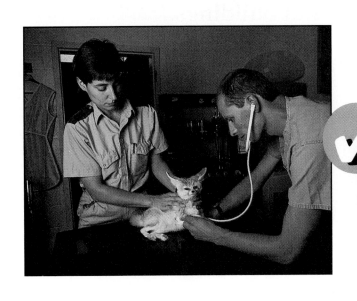

Why should people around the world work together to solve problems?

SKILLS
How To

Tell What Might Happen

People everywhere sometimes need help from other people. If you know what might happen, you can plan ways to help other people.

These pictures show a flood. A flood can be caused by rain that comes so fast and so heavy that water covers streets and buildings.

1. If people think the rain will cause a flood, how can they get ready?

2. Think about all the things that can happen if there is a flood. How can people help each other?

3. What can you do to help people in a flood far away?

Think and Do

What if there is supposed to be a snowstorm? Why would it be important to know what might happen?

Kids Meeting Kids

All children should have what they need. They should have food, clean water, and a safe home.

Kids Meeting Kids is a group that helps children get the things they need. Children and adults march to make life better for all children. They write letters to our country's leaders. They ask our leaders to make laws that protect children.

People who belong to Kids Meeting Kids also write to children in other countries. They are called pen pals for peace. Kids Meeting Kids wants to bring peace and fairness to all children.

What Can You Do?

- Write to Kids Meeting Kids to find out how you can help.
- Join a pen pal club and learn about children in other countries.

Story Cloth

Look at the pictures. They will help you remember what you learned.

Talk About the Main Ideas

1. The world is home to many different and interesting people.
2. Our faraway neighbors live, play, and work much like we do.
3. We trade goods with people around the world.
4. People everywhere are learning to get along.

Give a Speech   You are the President meeting with leaders from other countries. Tell them why people everywhere need to get along.

Review

Use Vocabulary

Which word goes with each line?

continent   **globe**   **world**   **language**

1. a model of the Earth

2. another name for the Earth

3. one of the largest bodies of land on the Earth

4. the words people use

Check Understanding

1. What country would you like to visit? Why?
2. On which continent is the country you want to visit? How would you get there?
3. How are children all over the world alike? How are they different?
4. Where are the North and South poles?

Think Critically

What is a problem that people all over the world are working to solve? Why?

How to Use a Bar Graph

Jamie got new clothes for school. Each block on the bar graph stands for one piece of clothing.

Jamie's New Clothes					
United States					
Canada					
China					

0   1   2   3   4   5

1. Which country made the greatest number of Jamie's new clothes?
2. Which country made the fewest?
3. How many of Jamie's new clothes were made outside of the United States?

Read More About It

This Is the Way We Go to School by Edith Baer. Scholastic. This book tells about some ways that children around the world get to school.

GLOSSARY

A

address

A way to find a home or building. (page 30)

apartment

One kind of home. (page 29)

B

bar graph

A picture that shows how many or how much. (page 160)

C

change

Something that happens to make things different. (page 32)

choice

What people pick instead of something else. (page 45)

city

A large community where people live, work, and play. (page 62)

community

A place where people live and the people who live there. (page 62)

continent

One of the largest bodies of land on the Earth. (page 152)

country

A land and the people who live in that land. (page 116)

D

diagram

A drawing that shows the parts of something. (page 140)

direction

North, south, east, and west. (page 68)

F

factory

A place where things are made. (page 96)

family

A group of people who care for one another. (page 28)

farm

A place where people raise food and other resources. (page 94)

flag

A symbol that stands for a country. (page 114)

forest

A place where many trees grow. (page 92)

G

globe

A model of the Earth. (page 152)

goods

Things that people make or grow. (page 70)

group

A number of people gathered together. (page 14)

H

hero

A person who is known for doing something special. (page 127)

hill

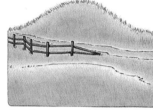

High land that is not as high as a mountain. (page 89)

holiday

A time to celebrate. (page 51)

J

job

The work a person does. (page 11)

L

lake

A body of water that has land around it. (page 89)

language

The words people use. (page 154)

law

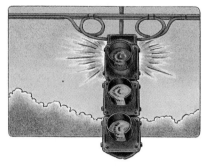

A rule that everyone must follow. (page 130)

leader

The person who helps a group plan what to do. (page 66)

learn

To find out something new. (page 6)

M

map

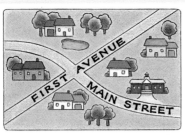

A drawing that shows where places are. (page 9)

map key

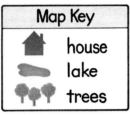

A list of the symbols that are used on a map. (page 12)

money

Coins or bills that people trade for things they want. (page 44)

mountain

The highest kind of land. (page 89)

N

needs

Things people cannot live without. (page 28)

neighborhood

A small part of a community. (page 62)

O

ocean

A very large body of salty water. (page 89)

P

pictograph

A picture that uses symbols to show numbers of things. (page 100)

plain

Land that is mostly flat. (page 89)

planet

A body in space, like the Earth, that moves around the sun. (page 162)

President

The leader of the United States. (page 127)

R

recycle

To make something old into something new. (page 102)

resource

Something people use that comes from the Earth. (page 92)

river

A long body of water that flows through the land. (page 89)

rule

What you must or must not do. (page 18)

S

school

A place for learning. (page 5)

services

Jobs that people do to help others. (page 66)

state

A part of a country. (page 116)

symbol

A picture that stands for something real. (page 12)

T

table

How Much We Weigh	
Name	Weight
Fred	48 lbs.
Juan	61 lbs.
Pete	53 lbs.

A list of things in groups. (page 72)

teacher

A person who helps people learn. (page 5)

time line

A line that shows when things happened. (page 42)

V

vote

A choice that gets counted. (page 128)

W

wants

Things people would like to have. (page 44)

world

A name for the Earth and everything and everyone on it. (page 150)

Unit 6:

Harcourt Brace & Company: 146 (r) Victoria Bowen; 148-149 (all) Victoria Bowen; 150 Terry D. Sinclair; 161 (t) Terry Sinclair; 162-165 (all), Brad Doherty

Other: 146-147 (spread) Bob Daemmrich/Stock, Boston; 147 (b) Donald Dietz/Stock, Boston; 151 (b) PhotoEdit; 151 (tl) SuperStock; 151 (tr) TSW; 151 (cl) PhotoEdit; 154 Charlene Daley/Valan Photos; 155 (t) Betty Press/Woodfin Camp & Associates; 155 (b) George Chan/Tony Stone Images; 156 (t) Superstock; 156 (b) FPG; 158, 159 Trade Commission of Mexico; 161 (tc) Tracy Pechette; 161 (bc) Tracy Pechette; 166 Vince Streano/Tony Stone Images; 167 (l) Richard Gaul/FPG; 167 (r) Bob Firth/International Stock Photo; 168-169 Kids Meeting Kids

Cover Credit:
Keith Gold & Associates

All maps by GeoSystems

Story Cloth Illustration Credits:

Unit 1
20-21, Lynne Cravath

Unit 2
54-55, Anni Matsick

Unit 3
80-81, Larry McEntire

Unit 4
108-109, Stacey Schuett

Unit 5
142-143, Carolyn Croll

Unit 6
170-171, Viv Eisner-Hess

For permission to reprint copyrighted material, grateful acknowledgment is made to the following sources:

Atheneum Books for Young Readers, Simon & Schuster Children's Publishing Division: America the Beautiful by Katharine Lee Bates, illustrated by Neil Waldman. Illustrations copyright © 1993 by Neil Waldman.

Curtis Brown Ltd.: "Good Books, Good Times!" from *Good Books, Good Times* by Lee Bennett Hopkins. Text copyright © 1985 by Lee Bennett Hopkins. Published by HarperCollins Publishers.

Harcourt Brace & Company: Flower Garden by Eve Bunting, illustrated by Kathryn Hewitt. Text copyright © 1994 by Eve Bunting; illustrations copyright © 1994 by Kathryn Hewitt.

Random House, Inc.: "Home! You're Where It's Warm Inside" from *The Random House Book of Poetry for Children* by Jack Prelutsky. Text copyright © 1983 by Jack Prelutsky.

Schroder Music Co.: Lyrics from "I Live in a City" by Malvina Reynolds. Lyrics © 1960 Schroder Music Co. (ASCAP), renewed 1988.

Viking Penguin, a division of Penguin Books USA Inc.: Cover illustration by Tracey Campbell Pearson from *School Days* by B. G. Hennessy. Illustration copyright © 1990 by Tracey Campbell Pearson.

Wonderland Music Company, Inc.: Lyrics and music from "It's a Small World" by Richard M. Sherman and Robert B. Sherman. Copyright © 1963 by Wonderland Music Company, Inc.; copyright renewed.